I BUILT ME

Conceptualizing Success in the 21st Century

Alfredo Salituro

Hardcover ISBN 978-1-7771251-0-3
Electronic Version ISBN 978-1-7771251-1-0

Hardcover 1st edition
July 2020

Book editor, Cassandra Filice
Book cover designer, David MacDonald

DEDICATION

I would like to dedicate this book to my sister Fiona Salituro, and to my parents Vincenza and Amedeo Salituro. Without you, I would not be where I am today.

I would also like to dedicate this book to all young, determined youth facing adversity beyond their control. The road forward may be difficult, and a light may seem far out of sight, but it can be reached. The ensuing journey will shape you; remember to use your unique perspective as a tool to build your own path. To build a better tomorrow.

CONTENTS

Preface | **vii**

Introduction | **ix**

Chapter 1 - Time is Finite | **1**

Chapter 2 - North Star | **7**

Chapter 3 - Breaking Barriers | **13**

Chapter 4 - Forming Relationships | **19**

Chapter 5 - Commitment to Persevere | **25**

Chapter 6 - Plan X, Y, Z | **31**

Chapter 7 - Opportunity | **37**

Acknowledgments | **43**

About the Author | **45**

Works cited | **47**

PREFACE

I Built Me is an accumulation of lessons and principles I have learned, observed, and practiced throughout my journey thus far. Having successfully overcome numerous challenges throughout both my personal life and professional career, I repeatedly found myself searching for answers to life's biggest questions. It is my wish to share my story, and to share the fundamental ideas and concepts I used to overcome life's adversities.

My goal was to create the book I was so desperately searching for during my time of need; to know that someone else had faced and overcome similar challenges, in hopes of helping others navigate their own adversity; for anyone asking themselves the same questions I once did.

To act as a guide, or even as a place to start.

INTRODUCTION

FINDING OUR PLACE in today's complex twenty first century certainty feels more challenging than any previous time throughout human history. With human evolution comes knowledge, expansion, growth, and exponentially more unanswered questions. Being fortunate to be able to build and expand on the knowledge of those who came before us provides a unique opportunity to carry forward with confidence and security. Today, one of the most common questions our generation continually asks is, "Where do we go from here?"

Having grown up in today's new technological era, and faced many roadblocks throughout my journey, I quickly realized I was not alone in my quest to build a better future. I consistently found myself trying to figure out why I am here and how can I make a difference. Millions of people like me are faced with challenges and questions for which answers seem forever out of reach.

This book sets out to create a guide and formulate a strategy to help all like-minded individuals who are trying to understand the world around them, and more important, trying to find their place in today's twenty-first century. Having grown up with a genetic blood disorder, and faced adversity on more than one occasion, I find myself in a unique position: I have successfully built myself into the person I always knew I could be, and I want to share how others can do the same, to help them push the boundaries of who we are as human beings and what we can collectively achieve.

"The ultimate paradox, of course, is that even though we're all going to die, we've all got to live in the meantime…" – Brian Cox

CHAPTER 1

TIME IS FINITE

THE MEANING OF life is different for everyone. It cannot be stumbled upon; it needs to be discovered. Regardless of one's journey, or circumstance in which we start, the process to find what we are all searching for is exactly the same. We need to remember that we are all human, brought here by distant stars and powers beyond our control. But we do have control: the control of our minds and ambitions.

Understanding the power we have to influence change in our lives and learning to manage our thoughts to our life circumstances will bring us the answers for which we are desperately searching.

So, where do we start? Or maybe the better question is, when did it all start? As of today, our best estimate tells us our universe was created around 13.8 billion years ago. Regardless if there was a creator or if the big bang was a random event, we cannot help but agree that we started somewhere. From that point on, "time" as we know it was created, and as far as human technology has reached, we still have not found a way to manipulate it. Since our creation, our minds have been free to imagine and hypothesize where our origins began and where our future is headed. As we ponder, we are cognizant of the ever-ticking clock, constantly reminding us of this finite, valuable gift.

For the time being, we must in essence embed the concept of time into our daily lives and use it as a guideline to build the framework of our lives. The more often we can recall the brevity of our time, the more successfully we can filter the activities on which we spend it. Time is truly our most limited and non-renewable resource, and we must be extremely careful with it. It is the one and only true currency we all have to spend.

Having been diagnosed with a genetic blood disorder at the age of three, I require regular blood transfusions every month of my life coupled with some at-home treatment. From a very young age, I remember being extremely aware of the concept of time. Not only the time I spent in the hospital, or the time dedicated to my treatment, but how rapidly time passes. I quickly realized that my body may not be able to carry me to the places and things I had been dreaming about. I regularly struggled with this realization as I watched my peers live their life in ways that I can't. Observing and comprehending my life around me in my teenaged years, I came to the conclusion that most people move through life unburdened by the thought of not having a tomorrow. Many of us take for granted what we have today, and it seems many of us are content with spending time recklessly, unaware of its importance.

I believe that recognizing the ephemeral element of time is a fundamental building block towards a successful and fulfilling life, and is thus why I chose to start my book with the concept of time.

I propose that the most successful people, those most driven and determined individuals, have built a strong and everlasting relationship with time. Whether they have been impacted directly or indirectly through a loved one's loss, or have come to the realization themselves, these people have made peace with time and this outlook shapes the way they navigate life. Having an almost poetic relationship with time is the first way to truly start building ourselves.

Having agreed time is finite and discovered a newfound appreciation for the time we do have on earth, the only obvious and reasonable next step would be to make the conscious choice not to waste it. We must set in motion our thoughts and feelings, those things, people, and ideas that make us who we are and define our humanity. To do this, we need to discover our catalyst.

A catalyst is a person or event that incites change. For example, throughout my childhood I had an extreme and profound love for aviation. Soaring in the sky and among the clouds was at the pinnacle of my tireless imagination. Observing the wonders of flight was my catalyst for a career in aviation. Your catalyst is something that makes you want to get up and move, or involuntarily causes you to perk up and sit a little taller in your chair at the sound of someone discussing the topic in the distance. It's what makes you, *you*.

We all have something that makes us unique; it can be very small or extremely big, a person, a place, or even a time period in our life. Anything for which we have a passion. Many people who do not believe they have a catalyst simply may not have had the opportunity to explore and discover what captures their attention. That doesn't mean that a catalyst does not exist for them.

It means we need to allocate more time to exploring ourselves and our own interests.

Moving forward with our new self-awareness of time, and having identified our catalyst that makes us unique, we can now slowly start piecing together the building blocks of our lives. The most important first step for any growth and personal development is the ability to appreciate the value of our life through the time we have. Being able to confidently identify who we are, and what makes us unique. It is only then we can build a picture of what we can be, and what we are truly capable of.

TIME IS FINITE: DISCOVER YOUR CATALYST

1. I enjoy doing

2. I like doing these activities because

3. I get excited when I think about

4. I would love to learn more about

5. 3 things I'm really good at are

6. If I could do anything in the world, it would be

"Its creative people who lead the vanguard forward into the unknown and transform the world." – Jordan B. Peterson

CHAPTER 2

NORTH STAR

FIRST, WE ACCEPT that time is finite. Then, we discover our catalyst, what inspires us. What next?

We take that catalyst and find our niche.

Extrapolating our catalyst into the real world will take some effort but will ultimately lead to an industry or a profession that falls within your interests. For example, if you have a passion for art, but you acknowledge that your own artistic abilities fall short, don't discard your passion or potential work in this field! You may be drawn to the world of art dealing. Or possibly becoming an entrepreneur and opening an art supply shop. This is the time to integrate and transform your catalyst into a career. It is also very important to mention that every catalyst, no matter how different or unique it might be, has some type of market and corresponding following. Somewhere in the world, someone wants something. There are customers for every product ever made, every service ever sold, and every experience ever offered. And if by chance your catalyst is something that has never been offered before, even better. You will have the opportunity to exploit your talent and potentially be the first to market.

We all have a place where we fit into the world and, despite the barriers we believe are set in front of us, everyone has something to offer.

Having dedicated time to locating and targeting a particular industry or profession, we must now filter through all the future pathway possibilities to find our north star.

Just as astronomers gaze into the vast emptiness of space, we too can sit back and stare into the unknown future looking for something to guide us. Our north star will be our guiding light, our end goal, our hopes and dreams. We must secure a point in the sky and fasten it in our minds to anchor our thoughts and help guide our daily decisions. This is most useful not only to get us to where we want to go, but to also help us spend our most valuable resource wisely: time.

The north star must not only be our end goal, but must also be achievable.

Up to this point we have cemented the foundation of our achievement timeline, today being our starting point, and our north star goal our desired end result. From this point forward, we can start filling in everything in between that must be accomplished in order to turn our north star goal into reality. Learning, creating, investing, inspiring…this is the time to lay out the framework.

As we all know, life never goes as planned. But we must still sketch an idea, *our* idea, into existence or else it can so easily be pushed aside or forgotten. If we have a north star and a plan to achieve it, we have created the building blocks of a success timeline. We can now start analyzing our environment to adapt and overcome the changes and barriers that may prevent us from reaching our full potential.

NORTH STAR: FIND YOUR NICHE

1. The 3 people who can help me are

2. I can find more information about my passion/ interest

3. 3 careers similar to the one I'm most interested in

4. I want this career/life style because

5. When I achieve my north star, I will feel

"Our destiny is not written for us; it's written by us."
– Barrack Obama, 44th President of the United States

CHAPTER 3

BREAKING BARRIERS

REFLECTING UPON THE environment in which we live is profoundly important. It helps us to better understand our current position in the world around us. Our environment has the potential to exponentially assist or hinder our ability to formulate an equation for success. The people and ideas we surround ourselves with most definitely start to influence and impact our trajectory. Much like creating a new timeline, every interaction and experience has the ability to alter our path ever so slightly. Over time, little quirks and inconveniences may magnify and manifest into barriers we must face later on, deeper into our journey, where they may be more difficult to remedy.

At this point it is easy to see where you are headed.

Surround yourself with the best people you possibly can.

Better still, the best place you can be to facilitate your success. Geographically, and philosophically, move yourself to an environment in which your north star and everything in between is protected. I call this re-routing your path.

The most important thing we need is to nurture our vision and create the person and the success that is defined by who we are.

Some things, however, cannot be changed, and some barriers are permanent and need to be addressed. Throughout my experience, every person I have ever met has at least one immovable barrier in their life. For the sake of simplicity, let's call it the 1% barrier. Our 1% is the things we cannot change, or a commitment we have made and must keep. For example, for me it was a medical condition, my commitment to my health. Despite my best efforts, and all the ancient herbal medicine and current scientific advances in this world, it is still the cards I have been dealt. Every person has faced some sort of adversity and those 1% barriers/commitments are the ones we cannot break and will need to put the extra effort into carrying them along with us.

At a very young age I had set my north star to become a fighter pilot in the Canadian military. Although my goal was ambitious, at my young age I failed to recognize my 1% barrier I would face down the road. My 1% barrier would eventually lead me to revisit my north star goal but not diverge from it completely. I believe in life, when facing adversity, it's easy to set our hopes and dreams aside, and forget who we are and can become for the easier and less impactful way out. It was extremely important to me that I was able to somehow incorporate aviation into the next stage of my life because it was my catalyst, it was who I am. My north star changed from military fighter pilot to aerospace engineer. I could live with the fact that if I couldn't fly at twice the speed of sound with my hair on fire, than at least I would be able to be a part of the aircraft creation.

This change at the time was madness. I had to leave flight school and retake courses at night school for an entire year just to be eligible for application to engineering programs. It was far more ambitious than I ever thought I would be able to achieve, but the most important fact was that it was aligned with my catalyst. It was who I was, and that drive is ultimately the most powerful engine we can have to propel us into the future.

Barriers are most easily broken when we are driven by passion and not greed.

Evaluating our own situation is something we all must do to break bad habits, re-route our path, and carry our 1%. With this comes clarity, and a sense of ease knowing we are facilitating the path of least resistance, and we are using our environment for us instead of against us.

BREAKING BARRIERS: OVERCOME OBSTACLES

1. My end goal is

2. My 3 biggest challenges to my goal right now are

3. I can overcome these challenges by

4. I can stay focused by

5. If my north star has to change, it could be

"If you are the smartest person in the room, you're in the wrong room." – Confucius

CHAPTER 4

FORMING RELATIONSHIPS

HELP: EVEN THE best of us need it. What better place to continue than with a firm grasp on the concept of time, a north star goal, and a handful of newly broken barriers in our wake.

This is the part in the story where we get to work, but we must not forget we are not alone. At some point, each of us will need to put our pride aside and ask for assistance.

Having evolved from the Stone Age to being on the cusp of quantum computing, we have built our modern day society as a team. To be more specific, a diverse team. If we wish to navigate the vastness of life in search of our purpose, we need to assemble a team that we can call upon to deliver fresh new ideas and lean on if needed.

Building a team affords us the ability to not only share burden but also strengthen and bolster our current and future trajectory. We need others for fresh ideas and perspectives, for new understandings and discoveries.

Second, the people with whom we share the most common interests and help facilitate our mindful development are the people who add fuel to our fire and allow our catalyst to burn hotter and brighter. Through our social network, the friends we meet throughout our journey have the ability to create a positive impact on our lives. The quality of the relationships we form vastly outweigh the quantity in our network. Aligning ourselves with the right people ultimately prevents the formation of barriers and nurtures the formation of strong and powerful bridges.

Forming relationships is somewhat of an easy task, such as meeting a new person at the office or being introduced by a mutual friend. The challenging part comes when we try to keep relationships strong and long lasting while our lives are continuously evolving. Every one of the 7.8 billion people currently living on earth is moving through life searching, exploring, yearning for the same answers; every one of them on a path crossing and intersecting yours along the way. It makes for a really messy social network and the best way I have found to deal with this conundrum is through consistency.

Not having the ability to dictate the actions,

thoughts, feelings, and directions of others consequently creates a delicate environment in which we must operate. On one hand, we must continue to build bridges and grow our network, while at the same time be able to safeguard our current relationships and prevent disruptive barriers from forming. We cannot predict who might become the next cornerstone in our lives or who may be gone within the week.

Proven consistency with regards to treating everyone equally, being reliable, and trustworthy, ultimately facilitates the path of least resistance. Being diligent enough to ensure our words match our actions will ensure the bonds and trust we do build in our relationships are never broken.

Once bonds are truly broken, they can be mended but will never return to what they once were. Consistency is the only option.

For the relationships that thrive, it's essential to know who will be able to guide you in times of uncertainty and illuminate your path, who will forever remember you and your character towards others.

And for that, and possibly that alone, the little extra time is most definitely worth spending.

FORMING RELATIONSHIPS: GATHER YOUR CIRCLE

1. 3 people I can depend on for support are

2. 3 people who inspire me are

3. 3 groups/committees I can join to help me achieve my goal are

4. 3 people I could reach out to for career guidance are

5. 3 qualities people have that I want to be around are

"You are the CEO of your life. Hire, fire, and promote accordingly." – Pawan Bansal

CHAPTER 5

COMMITMENT TO PERSEVERE

WHY SHOULD WE work towards a goal that encompasses the fundamental characteristics of who we are and what we are good at? What's the point? What does it mean?

Don't worry, we will get there. But now comes the hardest part. Making a commitment. A commitment precisely like a down payment on something that we do not fully understand. A commitment to ourselves, to the world, to the questions for which we don't have answers.

The commitment to us, for us, by us.
The commitment to persevere.

Understanding the personality traits that can be attributed to identifying a successful individual is a very difficult task. Many people and academic organizations believe intellectual ability such as qualitative and quantitative reasoning, or having an eidetic memory, is the most accurate identifier for selecting candidates who are deemed 'high potential.' Throughout my career I have been blessed to have met and interacted with many brilliant individuals with a high potential for success, each of whom has been filtered through hundreds of thousands of applicants using today's modern graduate school IQ tests.

However, the one dominant personality trait that is and will always be at the top of the success characteristic hierarchy, is grit.

The most influential trait that shapes ordinary people into leaders is often not measured. It's found in those people who came from low income families, in immigrants, children of immigrants, and in the people who have faced hardships and have learned sacrifice. Those are the people who, time and time again, lift up the people around them and finish at the top. Yes, being intelligent is very important. However, some of the most brilliant minds of our generations are usually extremely unmotivated. In my experience, you can only go so far in life relying on a strong memory or personality alone. Understanding the value of time, the sacrifice made by the people who came before us, goes far beyond the reach of any IQ test.

The silver lining of this story is that besides our upbringing, grit is a personality trait that can be taught, and learned, at any age.

We must be relentless in our pursuit and be determined to keep persevering even when we cannot see a light at the end of the tunnel. This is the same exact trait that makes the U.S. Navy Seals the most formidable force on the planet.

They. Do. Not. Quit.

Not for anything, not for anyone. If the mission is not complete, they will not quit. They will die before they quit. Although this comparison is indeed very extreme, it reinforces the commitment they make to each other, and themselves, to persevere despite the most extraordinary obstacles. This is the power of our minds, and grit is the key to unlocking all of our untapped potential we each have inside.

The path we take towards our north star goal is in most cases different from the path we intended to follow. The commitment to persevere affords us the ability to be situationally aware of our ever-changing environment, changing relationships, and network, allowing us to adapt and continue forward.

To the countless young, talented, ambitious individuals who will be forced to jump through never-ending hoops to prove their worth as I once did…

Keep going.

There is a way to get you to where you want to go, and it might not be the way you thought you would get there. There is always another way, another person to talk to, another opportunity to create. Build a way.

COMMITMENT TO PERSEVERE: STAY MOTIVATED

1. 3 ways I can stay motivated are

2. 3 ways I can stay healthy are

3. The steps I need to stay on track are

4. My short term goal and prospective goal date is

5. My long term goal and prospective goal date is

"You are always one decision away from a totally different life." – Unknown

CHAPTER 6

PLAN X, Y, Z

LIFE SELDOM GOES the way we draw it up. Even the best planners and the most detail-oriented professionals cannot dictate the series of events in which life will unfold. There are far too many variables to consider, let alone how the actions and intentions of others will inevitably affect us.

Navigating life is one of those peculiar situations where an outline, or even a rough sketch, is actually more useful than the entire painted picture.

Having lived the first 27 years of my life in North America, I became accustomed to the hustle and bustle mentality we have all willingly or unwillingly ingested. With my north star shining brightly and my commitment to persevere permanently cemented in my brain,

I took what was at the time the largest leap of faith of my life thus far: I moved to Europe. This milestone, although enormously complex, helped me understand the final steps to the recipe of success.

Despite having to deal with studying for the dreaded graduate entrance exam, while also working full time as an engineer, my road to graduate school was far more daunting than your average student's. My 1% barrier made sure I would have to earn every inch forward. Moving halfway across the world posed some logistical issues for me, especially being required to rely on routine hospital treatment. This greatly limited my ability to travel, and significantly reduced the university pool from which I was able to select. Once I completed my undergraduate degree in Canada, I began working in the United States, continuously traveling back to Canada every month for treatment. My 1% inconvenience started to become an exponentially greater burden standing between me and my future goals.

Then things changed. All my efforts started to pay off, and the pieces started falling into place. I was fortunate enough to have received dual citizenship from my parents and I was able to apply to graduate school in Italy. This opportunity opened an entire new world for me. With my goal to become a future industry leader, and my ambition at its highest levels, I set my sights on the top business school. As a result of many exam attempts, and countless nights working, studying, eating alone with only my commitment to persevere…I got in.

Since then, I have had opportunities I never thought possible. I have been blessed with the freedom to explore the world and continue my journey while building myself along the way.

From my dream of becoming a fighter pilot in the Royal Canadian Air Force, to being forced to withdraw from flight school, to taking a year off to retake high school academic courses, to fighting my way to becoming a private pilot, to conditional acceptance into university for a general science degree until I could prove my worth and commence engineering, to starting a semester behind my peers and spending every summer taking courses to catch up to my class, to graduating as an aerospace engineer in 3.5 years with an extra semester in science, and finally, to working as an engineer and earning an MBA from a top business school, and here, now, to becoming a self-published author…My path was absolutely nothing like what I had intended or expected.

Almost every plan I ever made failed. Using every failed path as newly gathered information, I consistently continued to create new plans of attack until eventually a few plans succeeded. Those victories made every failed attempt worth it.

As it stands today, I am on plan X or Y. To be honest I have lost count. But my commitment never faltered, never wavered in the face of uncertainty or adversity. The commitment to push, and the grit to stay the course was what ultimately made me successful.

This is the message I wish to share.
Always have another plan, plan B,
C, D….However many it takes.

PLAN X,Y,Z:
KNOW YOUR ALTERNATIVES

1. 1 crazy thing I could do to make a change is

2. 3 opportunities that I would most like to have are

3. If a plan fails, I can

4. 3 ways to mitigate potential obstacles are

5. If it all goes south, this is okay because

"I have not failed. I've just found 10,000 ways that won't work." – *Thomas Edison*

CHAPTER 7

OPPORTUNITY

WHAT HAVE I learned throughout my journey thus far? And how can we extract the meaning of life from the recipe to build success?

- **Go with the flow.** Be comfortable with a certain amount of chaos. As life unfolds, our ability to situationally adapt and logically navigate ultimately dictates our probability of success.

- **Enjoy the moment.** Time is the most precious concept we have. We must cherish each moment and be thankful for the breaths we do have, and the world we must take care of.

- **Discover and embrace our uniqueness.** What makes us unique is what can add the most value. We must set goals for ourselves that align with who we are inside. Your north star is ultimately you. Who you are, and who you see yourself becoming.

- **Break the barriers that prevent us from fulfilling what makes us happy.** Protect your space and be relentless in the pursuit of a healthy, nurturing environment. Surround yourself with the people, places, and things that nurture your imagination, creativity, and humanity.
- **Form relationships with people from whom we can learn, love, and grow.** Our relationships are far more important than we realize. They will help sculpt us into who we will become, and our networks have the power to magnify our actions and circle the globe.
- **Make a commitment.** To yourself, to the world, and to the life you have been gifted. Stay your course and strive to become the best version of yourself.
- **Accept uncertainty.** It is the poetic romance of life. Without risk there would be no reward. Our life is special because it has an end.

So, what does it all mean?

When we strive to become the most successful version of ourselves, we start to create new, unknown opportunities.

Opportunity to evolve into something new, something better.

Opportunity that not only benefits us, but also the world around us.

Opportunity to appreciate the simple truth that we have the ability to cherish Life and everything we have right in front of us.

Opportunity that will continue to tirelessly push humanity forward into the future.

Opportunity that ultimately falls to us.

To *you.*

To leave the world a little bit better than the way it was.

OPPORTUNITY: NOTES TO MYSELF

1. My favourite part of this book is

2. I enjoyed this part because

3. I feel most inspired to

4. I can help others around me by

5. I can make a difference because

"We are all time travelers, journeying together into the future. But let us work together to make that future a place we want to visit." – Stephen Hawking

ACKNOWLEDGMENTS

From the bottom of my heart, I would like to sincerely thank all my family and friends who have continuously supported me throughout my journey thus far. Although my road has not been the most linear path, it has undoubtedly shaped me into the man I am today.

I would also like to formally acknowledge a few very important individuals. To my brother Peter Romeo, and to Marcel Lariviere, Callum Chhokar, Jason Lamptey, Tanny Tran, Tom McCormick, and Chris Reis, thank you for continuously encouraging and inspiring me. Without you I would not be the person I am today, and for that I am forever grateful.

Finally, I would like to thank every nurse, doctor, and medical professional who has ever helped me, keeping me healthy and allowing me the opportunity to thrive. Without your tireless efforts many of us would not have the opportunity to change the world. Thank you for giving us that chance.

ABOUT THE AUTHOR

Alfredo Amedeo Salituro
October 3rd, 1991
Toronto, Canada

Ivey School of Business, Western University
MBA International Exchange Program, '20
London, Canada

SDA Bocconi School of Management,
Bocconi University
MBA, Masters of Business Administration, '20
Milan, Italy

Faculty of Engineering, University of Windsor
BASc, Bachelor of Applied Science Mechanical Engineering with Aerospace Option, '16
Windsor, Canada

WORKS CITED

BrainyQuote. Thomas A. Edison Quotes. https://www.brainyquote.com/quotes/thomas_a_edison_132683 Accessed 27 Jan. 2019.

Confucius, and Arthur Waley. *The Analects of Confucius.* New York: Vintage Books, 1938. Print.

Cox, Brian. *Why Does E=mc^2? (And Why Should We Care?).* Da Capo Press, 2010.

Hawking, Stephen. *Brief Answers to the Big Questions.* Thorndike Press, 2019.

Marvell, Andrew. *To His Coy Mistress.* Norton Anthology: English Literature. Ed. Julia Reidhead. United States: W. W. Norton And Company. 1990.

Obama, Barrack. "Remarks at a Campaign Rally." Denver, Colorado. 25 Oct 2012.

Peterson, Jordan. "Creativity is Foolish." *Facebook,* uploaded by Dr. Jordan B. Peterson 30 July, 2019, https://www.facebook.com/drjordanpeterson/videos/vb.1459175888057l8/2577519512259559/?type=2&theater.

YourQuote.in. Pawan Bansal. https://www.yourquote.in/pawan-bansal-ml42/quotes/you-ceo-your-life-hire-fire-promote-accordingly-luxo6. Accessed 27 Jan 2019.

CPSIA information can be obtained
at www.ICGtesting.com
Printed in the USA
LVHW081929090820
662765LV00018B/572/J

9 781777 125103